**Home Office Research Study 253**

# The road to ruin? Sequences of initiation into drug use and offending by young people in Britain

Stephen Pudney

*The views expressed in this report are those of the authors, not necessarily those of the Home Office (nor do they reflect Government policy).*

Home Office Research, Development and Statistics Directorate
December 2002

# Home Office Research Studies

The Home Office Research Studies are reports on research undertaken by or on behalf of the Home Office. They cover the range of subjects for which the Home Secretary has responsibility. Other publications produced by the Research, Development and Statistics Directorate include Findings, Statistical Bulletins and Statistical Papers.

## The Research, Development and Statistics Directorate

RDS is part of the Home Office. The Home Office's purpose is to build a safe, just and tolerant society in which the rights and responsibilities of individuals, families and communities are properly balanced and the protection and security of the public are maintained.

RDS is also part of National Statistics (NS). One of the aims of NS is to inform Parliament and the citizen about the state of the nation and provide a window on the work and performance of government, allowing the impact of government policies and actions to be assessed.

Therefore –

Research Development and Statistics Directorate exists to improve policy making, decision taking and practice in support of the Home Office purpose and aims, to provide the public and Parliament with information necessary for informed debate and to publish information for future use.

First published 2002
Application for reproduction should be made to the Communications and Development Unit, Room 201, Home Office, 50 Queen Anne's Gate, London SW1H 9AT.
© Crown copyright 2002    ISBN  1 84082 928.1
                          ISSN  0072 6435

# Foreword

This report presents an analysis of data from the 1998/99 Youth Lifestyles Survey (YLS), a representative sample of young people aged 12 to 30 living in England and Wales. It focuses upon the occurrence and timing of young people's first use of various types of illicit drugs and their first experience of various types of offending. Its aim is to test whether the data collected supports the 'gateway hypothesis', that the use of drugs, such as cannabis, increases the risk of future use of more harmful drugs, such as heroin and cocaine.

Using a range of statistical techniques to isolate the role of unobservable factors, this analysis concludes that true 'gateway' effects are probably very small. The author believes that the association between harmful and less harmful drugs found in survey data is spurious and largely the result of the difficulty of identifying and observing all the personal characteristics underlying individual drug use.

The data presented in this report are important in assessing the possible impact of the proposed re-classification of cannabis from class B to class C in late 2003. From the author's viewpoint, the decision to reclassify cannabis seems unlikely to have damaging future consequences in terms of leading young people to progress on to those more harmful drugs. Gateway effects are probably too small to be a major factor in the design of anti-drug policy. Furthermore, the author states that instead approaches, such as education, treatment and enforcement strategies are more likely to be effective.

DAVID PYLE
Assistant Director, Research, Development and Statistics Directorate

# Acknowledgments

I am grateful to the Home Office for the initial funding for this research and for providing access to the 1998/99 Youth Lifestyles Survey data. Three anonymous referees and participants at the 2002 Royal Economic Society conference in Warwick made valuable comments. Any errors are mine, as are the views expressed here.

Stephen Pudney
Department of Economics, University of Leicester

# Contents

The road to ruin? Sequences of initiation into drug use and offending by young people in Britain

# Summary

This is a study of the occurrence and timing of young people's first use of various types of illicit drug and their first experience of various types of offending, including truancy. Its aim is to investigate the gateway effect – the hypothesis that use of soft drugs leads to a higher future risk of hard drug use and crime.

The study makes use of information from the 1998/99 Youth Lifestyles Survey (YLS), which yields a set of around 3,900 interviews in which young people make a confidential report of their own experience of drug use and offending. They do this, unobserved by any other individual, by responding to questions generated automatically on the screen of a laptop computer.

On the surface, the YLS data seem broadly consistent with some variants of the gateway theory, in the sense that the age of onset for most soft drugs is less than the age of onset for most hard drugs. For example, the average age of first use of glue/solvents and cannabis are 14.1 and 16.6 years respectively, compared with 17.5 and 20.2 years for heroin and cocaine. However, there are anomalies: for example ecstasy has an average age of onset of 18.9 years compared to 17.5 years for heroin.

There is much less evidence of a gateway effect for drugs into crime. The average age of onset for truancy and crime are 13.8 and 14.5 years respectively, compared with 16.2 for drugs generally and 19.9 years for hard drugs. Thus crime tends to precede drug use rather than vice versa.

These links are investigated at the individual level, allowing for the influence of gender, ethnicity, family background, location, age and the prevalence of drug 'culture' in society at large. Superficially, this more detailed analysis still suggests a pattern of responses roughly consistent with the gateway hypothesis.

However, this conclusion could be unreliable. Suppose, for example, that a difficult family and social background predisposes a young person towards 'antisocial' behaviour. Soft drugs and minor crime offer the easiest avenues for the very young to offend but opportunity widens with age, so we tend to find an association between early soft drug use and later hard drug use. But, in this example, the association is at least partly spurious. Early soft drug use and later hard drug use may be joint expressions of the same underlying personal problem rather than a consequence of a causal influence of soft drug use on the subsequent desire for harder drugs. The apparent progression from soft to hard drugs may be just a consequence of the fact that soft drugs are easier to get and more affordable than hard drugs for the very young.

There are statistical techniques available to isolate the role of unobservable factors (such as a social or psychological predisposition towards antisocial behaviour) and thus solve this problem of spurious association. These methods work by trying to infer each individual's underlying predisposition from his/her general tendency towards early or late onset.

After applying these methods, there is very little remaining evidence of any causal gateway effect. For example, even if soft/medium drugs (cannabis, amphetamines, LSD, magic mushrooms, amyl nitrite) could somehow be abolished completely, the true causal link with hard drugs (crack, heroin, methadone) is found to be very small. For the sort of reduction in soft drug use that might be achievable in practice, the predicted causal effect on the demand for hard drugs would be negligible. Although there is stronger evidence of a gateway between soft drugs and ecstasy/cocaine, it remains small for practical purposes.

My interpretation of the results of this study is that true gateway effects are probably very small and that the association between soft and hard drugs found in survey data is largely the result of our inability to observe all the personal characteristics underlying individual drug use. From this viewpoint, the decision to reclassify cannabis seems unlikely to have damaging future consequences.

**Introduction**

Rising trends in truancy, crime and illicit drug use by young people constitute one of the most important social developments of the post-war world. A particularly disturbing aspect of this development is the trend towards earlier onset of these patterns of behaviour. Public policy has responded to these alarming trends and, in Britain, the government has adopted an ambitious target of reducing the availability and use by young people of certain types of drug by 25 per cent by 2005 and 50 per cent by 2008 (UKADCU, 2000). Similar targets apply to the level of drug-related crime. However, effective anti-drugs policy may need to go beyond general targeting of this kind to much more specific action. If there is indeed a slippery slope from early minor offending through soft drugs to hard drugs and serious crime, then the question must be asked whether there are critical stages in this causal chain, against which policy is best directed. This has become an urgent question, given recent moves towards a more relaxed policy on cannabis: particularly the recent recommendation by the Advisory Council on the Misuse of Drugs (2002) for the reclassification of cannabis to class C status and the apparently successful experiment in more permissive policing of cannabis possession in Lambeth (Metropolitan Police Service, 2002). Some commentators are worried that a more liberal stance on soft drugs will open the door to more dangerous forms of drug use for people who, until now, have been deterred by the strong line on cannabis.

Policy initiatives are presently based on quite limited knowledge of the behaviour underlying the rising trend in drug use. The most important unresolved issue is the existence and size of the 'gateway' effect. Gateway theory holds that the act of consuming a soft drug such as cannabis causes an increase in the risk of becoming a hard drug user. There are several ways in which a gateway effect might come about. Firstly, the act of obtaining and using soft drugs may bring the user into contact with hard-drug users or suppliers whom they would not otherwise have met. Secondly, the consumption of soft drugs may create a psychological or physiological need for further, stronger experiences of the same type. Thirdly, experience of the use of soft drugs with no obvious ill effects may appear to contradict and undermine the strong negative publicity directed against illicit drugs in general, so that advice against hard drugs becomes less persuasive. Fourthly, some individuals may be driven towards risky or illegal activities, either as a way of obtaining respect from their peers, or as a way of consuming 'excitement'. A rising general level of soft drug use then raises the stakes, so that resort to hard drugs becomes necessary to achieve this sort of respect or excitement.

1   See Stratford and Roth (1999) and Flood-Page *et al.* (2000) for discussion of the evidence on this in the UK context.

For policy purposes it is important to bear in mind the different ways in which gateways may arise. Gateway theory is often, quite wrongly, assumed to give automatic support to strict policies on drugs. Suppose gateway effects arise through induced social contacts with undesirable influences, or through the undermining of anti-drugs advice. Then a more liberal policy, which tends to drive a wedge between sources of soft and hard drug supply and to differentiate the perceived advice on soft and hard drugs, could plausibly be argued to reduce rather than increase the numbers of people moving on to hard drugs.

An important first step is to investigate the existence and size of gateway effects. It is not easy to do this. Illicit behaviour is inherently difficult to observe in any systematic way and real understanding will require a complementary mix of intensive qualitative research, case studies and general-population survey-based research. The aim of the present study is to contribute to the last of these strands of research and estimate the strength of the gateway effect, using recent British survey data. However, reliance on large-scale surveys requires some justification. Individuals with the most serious drug and offending behaviour are inevitably under-represented in surveys of the general population, since they are less likely to participate in voluntary survey enquiries. The competing demands on questionnaire content, the misreporting of sensitive information and imperfect recall of past events all combine to make survey data less deep, less informative and less reliable than one would like. Nevertheless, there is no other way of gathering detailed information representative of the range of behaviour displayed by a large part, if not all, of the population of young people.

There is enormous variety in patterns of 'problem' behaviour. In particular, drug use can vary greatly over time and across individuals. Periods of intensive use may alternate with periods of remission. Some people may experiment briefly with drugs or crime and then stop permanently. At the moment, the UK has no large-scale longitudinal survey that can follow individuals through time, observing the evolution of their offending and drug use. This is in contrast with the American National Longitudinal Study of Youth, which goes some way towards meeting this need. In the absence of a major longitudinal study, survey work must necessarily be of more limited scope since it is not possible to observe drug use and offending in full detail. Instead, this study focuses on only one aspect of drug/offending careers, the age of onset. Thus the key question is the timing of initiation into various types of drug use or offending, without considering the subsequent rate and pattern of use. This is, of course, only a partial view of drug and offending careers, justified in part by necessity, driven by the paucity of reliable information. But the author would go further and argue that the age of onset is a critical aspect, meriting particular attention. It is trivially obvious that there can be no drug problem if there is no first use of drugs, so onset is always an important event. There is also compelling evidence that early onset is strongly associated with later high-risk behaviour. For example, Kandel and Yamaguchi (1993) found evidence of early onset as a risk factor for progression to the more dangerous illicit drugs. Van Ours (2002) and Pudney (2002), dealing respectively with alcohol and tobacco and with cannabis, found a strong link between early onset and the volume of subsequent consumption. Note also that Pudney (2002) found the expected long-term impact of early onset to be large despite the existence of a sizeable group who experiment briefly without becoming regular users (see also Aldridge *et al.* (1999) for evidence on this group).

Even with very detailed longitudinal data, it would be hard to resolve the dynamic causal structure underlying observed sequences of initiation to different types of offending and drug use. The reason for this is that it is not possible to do controlled social experiments. The author would like to be able to investigate the impact of the early use of (say) cannabis by observing a control group with normal exposure to all 'vices' except cannabis and then comparing their lifecourse outcomes with those of a treatment group who are given additional exposure to cannabis. With random allocation to the control and treatment groups, this comparison would give very persuasive evidence on the true causal role of cannabis within the developmental process of offending and drug use. When experimentation is not possible, individuals are not assigned to groups, but rather select themselves into the 'control' group (non-users of cannabis) and the 'treatment' group (cannabis users).

To illustrate the difficulty caused by non-random allocation, assume for the sake of argument that there is no true gateway effect. In other words, taking cannabis does not increase one's risk of becoming a hard drug user. However, assume that there may exist personal factors of some kind that could predispose a child towards 'problem' behaviour generally. Examples might include a disturbed family background or some kind of psychological disorder. A seriously affected child is likely to be at different times a truant, an offender and a user of various illicit drugs. Now assume further that the opportunities for different kinds of problem behaviour tend to arise at different points in life. This may come about in several ways. Relative cost may be responsible; cocaine is more expensive than cannabis and children tend to have little available money, so it is likely that cannabis will be affordable earlier than cocaine. Similarly, truancy and petty crime, which require no resources, are also likely to occur relatively early. Differences in availability may have a similar effect; cannabis is more available than cocaine, so even if cost is not a consideration, someone who sets out to experience drugs will, on average, find an opportunity to take cannabis before an opportunity to take cocaine[2].

---

2   These arguments seem plausible in the light of Table 2.1 below which suggests that behaviours with a very low 'cost per use' and wide availability (crime, truancy, solvents, tobacco, alcohol) typically have early onset, while the more expensive hard drugs tend to occur later.

This combination of two factors, a generalised predisposition towards all forms of problem behaviour and externally induced differences in the typical timing of events, will tend to produce systematic sequences of outcomes. Young people will tend to start their problem careers with truancy and crime and soft drugs, then move on to increasingly serious drug use. A casual observer might then be led to conclude that there is a stepping stone or gateway effect from earlier, mild, forms of problem behaviour to later, more serious, forms of problem behaviour. Yet, in this hypothetical case, the casual observer would be quite wrong; these systematic career paths have arisen without any true causal link from one kind of drug use to another. Thus researchers face a difficult problem in trying to separate causal gateway effects from the spurious empirical association produced by other common underlying factors[3].

There are three main approaches to the difficult problem of disentangling causal and non-causal sources of empirical association. The most common approach in early research was to avoid the issue by presenting statistical evidence on the strength of empirical association between soft drugs and then (implicitly or explicitly) leaving its causal significance as a matter of interpretation. A second approach is to try to eliminate all the factors responsible for producing spurious empirical associations by designing special surveys that give greater depth of information on the social and psychological circumstances influencing each individual's behaviour. These variables are then used to control for the effects of confounding factors. Influential examples of this approach include Yamaguchi and Kandel (1984a, 1984b) and Fergusson and Horwood (2000)[4].

A third approach is motivated by the view that no survey information, however detailed, can capture all of the individual-specific confounding factors that might be at work. Consequently, methods have been developed which allow for the presence of such factors without requiring direct observation of them. These methods are based on the idea that, if there is some fundamental factor that predisposes an individual towards 'problem' behaviour, then it is likely to display two characteristics. Firstly, it will tend to be stable and persistent over time; and secondly, it will have an impact reflected simultaneously in a wide range of behavioural aspects. By observing an individual's broad pattern of behaviour over

3   This type of problem is very common and is often responsible for apparently perverse empirical associations. For example, it is an empirical fact that there is a high death rate among hospital inmates. Does this mean that medical practice should be banned? Clearly not, the apparent negative relation between medical attention and high mortality is the result of neglecting a common underlying factor. People receiving medical attention tend to be ill and people who are ill tend to have higher mortality risk. Unless one can control for the confounding factor of illness, it is impossible to assess the true causal impact of medical attention on mortality risk.

4   There are dangers in this approach. It is particularly important to make sure that the socio-psychological variables are indicators of fundamental factors rather than mere symptoms of problem behaviour. For example, a difficult parent-child relationship or difficulties at school may be symptoms rather than causes of problem behaviour by the child.

time and comparing it with the behaviour typical of others, it becomes possible to isolate the individual-specific confounding factor and assess its contribution to the empirical association between minor offending/drug use and subsequent more serious problem behaviour. Thus, unobservable confounding factors are identified indirectly from the nature of their impact rather than directly by observation. This approach, which takes account of the 'unobservable heterogeneity' of individuals is used in many areas of statistics but has seen little application so far in the analysis of drug use and offending. Exceptions include panel data regression analysis by economists focusing on the impact of price variation on drug consumption (see Kenkel *et al.* (2001) for a survey) and a recent study of Amsterdam data on the cannabis-cocaine gateway by Van Ours (2001) who used transition modelling techniques.

This study also uses a transition model extended to allow for unobservable confounding factors, in an attempt to assess the true gateway association that remains after extracting the influence of persistent individual-specific factors. In addition to implementing this approach on British data, the study aims to extend the scope of gateway analysis by examining a broad spectrum of problem behaviour, including truancy, minor offending and more serious criminal activity. In principle, gateways can exist (in either direction) between crime and drugs as well as between soft drugs and hard drugs.

# 2    A picture of drug use and offending: The 1998/99 Youth Lifestyle survey (YLS)

The 1998/99 YLS is an extended version of a youth survey first conducted in 1993. It covers the 12 to 30 age group, who were identified through one or other of two methods. A core sample of 3,643 young people was identified from households participating in the 1998 British Crime Survey (BCS). This sample was then topped up. The occupants of addresses adjacent to those of the core sample were screened to identify more subjects in the target age group. To ensure adequate coverage of high-crime areas, this top-up sample was deliberately biased towards areas identified by the BCS as having high victimisation rates. This over-sampling raised the coverage of high-crime areas from 27.5 per cent in the core sample to 35.4 per cent in the top-up sample.

Fieldwork took place between October 1998 and January 1999. Interviewing was subject to written consent from the parents of subjects aged under-16. Face-to-face computer assisted personal interviewing (CAPI) and computer assisted self interviewing (CASI) were used for different parts of the data gathering process, with CASI employed for the sensitive topics of drug use and criminal activity. The response rate was 69.1 per cent, yielding a final usable sample of 3,901 respondents[5]. Further detail on the design and conduct of the survey can be found in Stratford and Roth (1999) and Flood-Page *et al.* (2000). The YLS questionnaire gives considerable detail on respondents' family circumstances, both currently and at age 15. Many aspects of experience at school are also recorded. Appendix Table A1 summarises the variables used to describe individual characteristics and family background.

The focus of this study is on drug use and its relation to truancy and criminal activity. Drug use is here interpreted broadly to cover each of a set of 12 illicit substances together with consumption of alcohol and tobacco[6]. Importantly for these purposes, the questionnaire asks for the age at which each of these substances was first consumed. The basic sample characteristics of the age of onset for each category are summarised in Table 2.1. Three summary statistics are given for each drug: the sample percentage reporting any previous

---

5   Altogether there were 4,848 respondents. However, a randomly-selected comparison group were administered the drug/offending questionnaire by paper-based personal interviewing (PAPI) rather than CASI. Data on this latter group has not been used to avoid the more serious under-reporting that appears to occur under PAPI.

6   The YLS also contains questions about a non-existent drug 'semeron', included to test response reliability and questions about anabolic steroids. The number of respondents claiming experience of semeron is very small and such cases have been dropped. Anabolic steroids have been excluded from the analysis because of the very low level of prevalence and the rather different use to which steroids are put.

use; the mean age of first use for those who had used the drug; and the proportion of users who had begun before their 16th birthday. All of these statistics are weighted to be representative of the 12 to 30 age group in the population[7].

A fairly clear pattern emerges from Table 2.1. The drugs with earliest onset, around age 14, are alcohol, tobacco and glue/solvents. Over three-quarters of the people who report experience of these substances commenced use before the age of 16. There is then a gap of around 2 years before the mean age of first use of cannabis and amyl nitrite. A little later, at age 17-18, comes the first use of hard drugs (heroin and crack) and other substances (amphetamines, LSD, mushrooms, tranquillisers). The most 'adult' drugs are methadone, ecstasy and finally cocaine, which has a mean age of first use of almost 20. There seems to be some support here for a division of drugs into five groups: (i) early onset legal substances (alcohol, tobacco); (ii) glue/solvents; (iii) early/middle onset soft drugs (amphetamines, cannabis, LSD, mushrooms, tranquillisers, amyl nitrite); (iv) early/middle onset hard drugs (heroin, crack, methadone); (v) late onset recreational drugs (ecstasy, cocaine).

---

7   For reasons of confidentiality, there is limited access to survey design details. Thus, it is not possible to identify each primary sampling unit, nor to link primary subjects with the associated focused enumeration subjects. Consequently, the confidence intervals in Tables 2.1 and 2.2 only take partial account of the sample structure, through the survey weights which attempt to adjust for non-response and the over-sampling of high-crime areas. The confidence intervals should be regarded as approximate indicators of statistical precision and may over-estimate precision to some degree.

**Table 2.1    Prevalence, age of first use and frequency of early use by drug/offence type** (weighted estimates with 95% confidence bands)

| Event | Prevalence | Mean age of onset | % under 16 |
|---|---|---|---|
| Amphetamines | 19.7 ± 1.6 | 17.8 ± 0.3 | 22.1 ± 3.8 |
| Cannabis | 38.6 ± 1.9 | 16.6 ± 0.2 | 41.8 ± 3.2 |
| Cocaine * | 7.5 ± 1.1 | 20.2 ± 0.5 | 7.4 ± 4.3 |
| Crack * | 1.5 ± 0.5 | 18.4 ± 1.0 | 18.2 ± 12.0 |
| Ecstasy | 9.5 ± 1.2 | 18.9 ± 0.4 | 13.3 ± 4.8 |
| Heroin * | 1.2 ± 0.4 | 17.5 ± 0.9 | 25.2 ± 14.2 |
| LSD | 11.2 ± 1.3 | 17.2 ± 0.3 | 29.0 ± 5.7 |
| Magic mushrooms | 9.1 ± 1.2 | 17.3 ± 0.4 | 32.3 ± 6.2 |
| Methadone * | 0.7 ± 0.3 | 18.4 ± 1.6 | 23.2 ± 19.9 |
| Tranquillisers | 3.6 ± 0.7 | 18.2 ± 0.6 | 19.6 ± 7.5 |
| Amyl nitrite | 15.7 ± 1.5 | 16.9 ± 0.3 | 33.5 ± 4.8 |
| Glue/solvents | 7.8 ± 1.1 | 14.1 ± 0.3 | 83.2 ± 5.4 |
| Any drug | 42.7 ± 1.9 | 16.2 ± 0.2 | 47.6 ± 1.7 |
| Any hard drug | 8.1 ± 1.2 | 19.9 ± 0.5 | 11.2 ± 4.4 |
| Alcohol | 90.2 ± 1.1 | 13.8 ± 0.1 | 76.8 ± 1.7 |
| Tobacco | 71.4 ± 1.7 | 14.0 ± 0.2 | 76.4 ± 2.0 |
| Truancy | 32.1 ± 1.8 | 13.8 ± 0.1 | 67.9 ± 3.3 + |
| Minor crime | 43.4 ± 1.9 | 14.5 ± 0.3 | 69.0 ± 2.7 |
| Serious crime | 9.4 ± 1.2 | 14.5 ± 0.4 | 65.6 ± 6.3 |

* Member of 'hard' drug group; + % at age 14 or under for truancy

Crime is represented by participation in either of two groups of offences. The first is a group of 18 'minor' offences (criminal damage, arson, theft, dealing in stolen goods, cheque and credit card offences, fraud and public fighting) and nine 'serious' crimes (theft of vehicles, robbery, breaking and entering and assault). The full set of 27 offences identified by the YLS is given in Flood-Page et al. (2000, Appendix B). There is some evidence of a progression from truancy to minor crime to serious crime. This progression tends to occur early relative to most drug use.

The sequencing of drug use events within the larger process of offending and truancy behaviour is summarised in Table 2.2, which gives weighted sample frequencies of the logically possible event sequences. The two columns of Table 2.2 correspond to two alternative definitions of crime and drug use: the first covers all drugs (excluding alcohol and tobacco) and all crime; the second covers only hard drugs (cocaine, crack, heroin, methadone) and serious crime.

**Table 2.2**  **Sequences of illicit behaviour** (weighted estimates with 95% confidence bands)

| Sequence | % frequency (broad definition) | % frequency (serious crime & drugs only) |
|---|---|---|
| No offending or drug use | 34.9 ± 1.8 | 61.8 ± 0.9 |
| Truancy only | 6.3 ± 0.9 | 23.0 ± 1.6 |
| Crime only | 11.5 ± 1.1 | 3.2 ± 0.7 |
| Drugs only | 8.8 ± 1.1 | 2.6 ± 0.6 |
| Truancy➤drugs | 4.7 ± 0.7 | 3.3 ± 0.8 |
| Truancy➤crime | 2.8 ± 0.7 | 3.1 ± 0.7 |
| Crime➔drugs | 8.8 ± 1.1 | 0.1 ± 0.1 |
| Crime➔truancy | 2.5 ± 0.6 | 1.6 ± 0.5 |
| Drugs➔truancy | 1.7 ± 0.6 | 0.1 ± 0.1 |
| Drugs➔crime | 5.8 ± 1.0 | 0.2 ± 0.2 |
| Truancy➤crime➔drugs | 5.5 ± 1.0 | 1.5 ± 0.5 |
| Truancy➤drugs➔crime | 5.1 ± 1.0 | 0.5 ± 0.3 |
| Crime➔truancy➤drugs | 6.4 ± 1.0 | 0.5 ± 0.3 |
| Drugs➔crime➔truancy | 1.8 ± 0.5 | 0.1 ± 0.2 |
| Drugs➔truancy➤crime | 2.5 ± 0.7 | 0.1 ± 0.2 |
| Crime➔drugs➔truancy | 3.4 ± 0.7 | 0.1 ± 0.2 |
| Drugs➔truancy or crime | 11.8 ± 1.4 | 0.6 ± 0.5 |
| Crime➔truancy or drugs | 21.1 ± 1.8 | 2.3 ± 0.7 |
| Truancy➤drugs or crime | 17.9 ± 1.7 | 8.4 ± 1.2 |

Note: Tied events are double-counted; alcohol and tobacco are excluded

This simple tabulation exercise is revealing. There is a reasonably clear tendency towards a chain of events beginning with crime and truancy, and only later developing into drug use. Sequences of offending beginning with drug use have a significantly smaller sample frequency than sequences beginning with truancy or crime, and this is particularly true when considering only hard drugs and serious crime. If one were prepared to assume that this tendency has causal significance then this study might conclude that a policy addressing truancy and other problems at school might be more effective than a policy attacking drug use directly. This issue is now examined in more detail by developing empirical models of drug use and offending behaviour and their relationship to personal characteristics and circumstances.

# 3                                                   The methodological approach

A method of analysis is now developed that can analyse individual sequences of offending and drug use, isolating the effects of observable and unobservable explanatory factors. This is necessarily a very technical process, requiring advanced statistical techniques. This chapter gives an outline description of the approach. The details are set out in the Technical Appendix, sections A1 and A2.

## Transitions and hazards

There are two basic concepts underlying the analysis: transitions and hazards. When an individual first commits a particular crime or first uses a particular drug, he or she is making a *transition* from being a non-offender or non-user to being an offender or user. The aim is to analyse the timing of these transitions. Timing, here, means the age at which the transition occurs, rather than calendar time. Because human behaviour is imperfectly predictable, these transition times are partly random (at least as far as the outside observer is concerned). Consider a person who has not yet become a drug user. In any given period there is some probability that he or she will make the transition from non-user to user. This is known as the *hazard* rate associated with that particular transition at that particular time. It is defined as the probability of becoming a user during the period in question, conditional on past and present circumstances and on not already being a user. Hazard rates will vary a great deal between people. Some types of people (such as young males in deprived areas) are at greater risk than others of becoming users. For any individual, the hazard rate is also likely to vary with age. To accommodate variation of the hazard, this study relates it to personal characteristics, indicators of the evolving social and economic environment, and the individual's own past history of drug use and offending. For example, suppose a number of different categories of drugs and crime are identified and there is particular interest in the hard drugs category. The hazard of becoming a hard drug user at age *t* can be written in general terms:

$\Pr$(onset of hard drugs at age $t$ | no use of hard drugs before age $t$)

$$= P(d_t; x_t; A_t; u) \tag{1}$$

where: $d_t$ represents a set of qualitative variables indicating which other types of drug and criminal activity the individual has experienced prior to age $t$; $x_t$ represents a set of variables describing the individual and his or her environment at age $t$; $A_t$ is a variable describing the macro environment (for instance, an indicator of general prevalence); and $u$ represents all unobservable confounding factors. After allowing for the influence of $u$, the impact of the variables $d_t$ represent the true gateway effects of each of the other drug/crime types into hard drugs. With several different categories of drugs and crime, there is a gateway effect in each direction for every possible pair of categories[8].

This transition modelling is implemented in two different ways. The simplest approach is to model each type of transition separately, ignoring the possible unobservable characteristics $u$. For this purpose the study uses a probit model, which is analogous to the widely-used logistic regression model. An analysis of this kind is carried out separately for each of the different drug and offence types, treating each year of each respondent's life (up to and including the age of onset) as a separate observation. The method and resulting estimates are detailed in the Technical Appendix (section A1 and Table A1[a] to [f]). The variables used to describe the individual and his or her situation at each year of age are described in the next section.

The drawback of the simple one-drug-at-a-time analysis is that it fails to take account of the unobservable individual-specific factors $u$ that may have a persistent influence on hazards over time and across different types of drug/offence. To make allowance for such effects all types of hazard must be analysed simultaneously, allowing the hazards of different types of drug or offence and at different times to be correlated as a consequence of the underlying behavioural factors. The method is explained in detail in the Technical Appendix (section A2 and Table A2 [a] and [b]).

## The observable characteristics of individuals and their social environment

The observable characteristics used to describe the circumstances of YLS respondents are summarised in Table 3.1. The YLS is a cross-section survey with a modest amount of retrospective recall data. As a consequence, characteristics which summarise family background, and which are potentially variable over time, are only observable at one point in time. This reference period is defined as the time of the respondent's 15 year of age or the time of the survey, whichever is the earlier. These variables record whether or not the mother or father was absent from the family and also the employment status of each parent. Other variables,

8   In the multi-state case the hazard rates are more generally described as transition intensities. See Lancaster (1990) for an account of the multi-state transition model. Note that there is a curse of dimensionality here. If a very detailed 17-category analysis is attempted, there will be 17x16=272 logically possible gateways. Even the simplified 6-category analysis adopted subsequently entails 30 possible gateways. Some gateways are more interesting than others – for example, few observers believe there to be a significant gateway from prior heroin use to subsequent cannabis use.

describing the neighbourhood (inner city and/or socially deprived), family history of trouble with the police and any religious affiliation, are observable only at the time of interview.

Note that characteristics like educational achievement, employment status and earnings are not used in the analysis, because they are viewed as outcomes of the process of personal development, rather than extraneous causal factors. To use them as pure explanatory factors would risk serious bias if, in fact, educational and employment attainment are jointly determined together with the behaviour under study.

**Table 3.1    *Personal characteristics of YLS respondents***
(n = 3,901; weighted estimates with 95% confidence bands)

| Characteristic | Definition | YLS % frequency |
|---|---|---|
| Female | Female gender | 49.8 ± 1.9 |
| Asian | Indian, Pakistani or Bangladeshi ethnic origin | 4.4 ± 0.8 |
| Black | Afro-Caribbean, black African or other black ethnic origin | 1.8 ± 0.4 |
| Religious | Claims religious affiliation | 13.5 ± 1.3 |
| Absent father | Had no father at age 15 (or none currently if below 16) | 6.5 ± 0.9 |
| Absent mother | Had no mother at age 15 (or none currently if below 16) | 1.2 ± 0.3 |
| Working father | Father in work at age 15 (or currently if below 16) | 85.7 ± 1.3 |
| Working mother | Mother in work at age 15 (or currently if below 16) | 71.6 ± 1.7 |
| Family Trouble | Parents or other family members have been in trouble with police | 1.7 ± 0.5 |
| Inner City | Resident in inner-city area | 14.6 ± 1.2 |
| Deprived area | Resident in one of the eight most deprived wards covered by the 1998 British Crime Survey | 6.5 ± 0.8 |

The characteristics of the individual, family and neighbourhood give only part of the picture. The cultural environment and nature of the illicit drug market may be at least as important. There are two obvious issues to consider here. One is the impact on individuals of the growing social acceptance of drug use and availability of supply. Another is the trend in drug prices.

Social norms and interactions are difficult to define, identify and measure (see Manski (1993, 2000) and Brock and Durlauf (2000) for discussion of the technical issues involved). The best that can be done with the limited information available in the YLS is to use macro-level proxy variables to capture the changing levels of social acceptance and availability encountered by successive cohorts of young people. A separate study (Pudney, 2001) has constructed index numbers of market size for each of the principal illicit drugs, using time-series indicators of consumption and supply[9]. These indices are plotted in Figure 3.1 for the period 1978-1989 and in some cases (notably amphetamines, LSD and cannabis) follow paths that would be difficult to capture using simple time trends[10].

**Figure 3.1    Indices of drug availability (source: Pudney, 2001)**

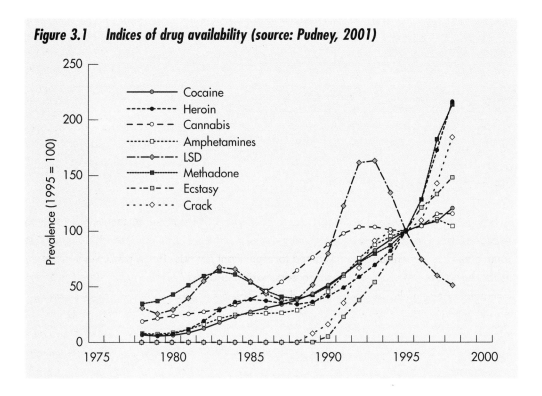

Drugs are goods like any other and it is likely that drug use is responsive to price variation. However, price effects raise difficult empirical problems. The available data on street prices of illicit drugs are sparse and not very reliable. They fall far short of the quality of a conventional price index and are only available in anything like a consistent form for the period since 1988. The nearest thing to an official source of information is the UK National Criminal Intelligence Service (NCIS), which produces unpublished tables giving rough

9   Up to six indicators were used for each drug: the number and volume of police drug seizures; the number and volume of Customs and Excise seizures, the number of drug-related convictions; and BCS prevalence rates.

10  The prevalence indices are used in log form in the econometric modelling. For crack and ecstasy, the study assumes a prevalence of 0.5% of the 1995 level prior to 1989, since the indicators of drug use were not published or were too low to permit estimation of prevalence. For the drug/offending categories not shown in Figure 3.1, quadratic time trends were used to capture the effect of changing conditions. When grouping drugs into broad categories, the indices for each constituent are weighted together by BCS prevalence rates. Note that the use of these indices gives a better statistical fit of the transition model than does the alternative of a quadratic trend.

ranges of typical street prices in a few particular locations. Figure 3.2 plots the NCIS price series in real terms for the London drug market[11].

There are two problems with these price data for the purposes of this study. Firstly, to incorporate price effects explicitly, would require a sequence of past prices covering the relevant past of people aged up to 30 in 1998. This entails price series going back to 1978, whereas only half of that period is available. Secondly, given the inherent unreliability of the data, it is not reasonable to infer more from Figure 3.2 than that there has been a steady downward trend in the real price of the major illicit drugs over the 1978-1998 period of roughly three per cent per year. It would be rash to attribute much significance to the year-to-year swings around this common trend. Moreover, although the NCIS prices are available for a few different locations, these do not cover the whole country and it is not possible to link YLS respondents to specific locations. Consequently, the geographical component of price variation cannot be used to identify price effects, even if one were prepared to trust it as a true measure.

A further issue is supply constraints. Drugs are illicit commodities which are not routinely available in the same way as other goods. It is very likely that many individuals in the YLS sample will have been supply constrained for significant periods. This is particularly important in the early part of their drug use careers, which are the focus of this study. Given the incomplete and unreliable price data and the unobserved but probably widespread quantity constraints on demand, there is little point in attempting a standard type of demand analysis with explicit use of price variables. Instead, the study relies on the constructed prevalence indices to act as proxies for consumption externalities, availability and also price movements.

11  To construct Figure 3.2, the mid points of quoted price ranges have been taken and deflated by the Retail Price Index.

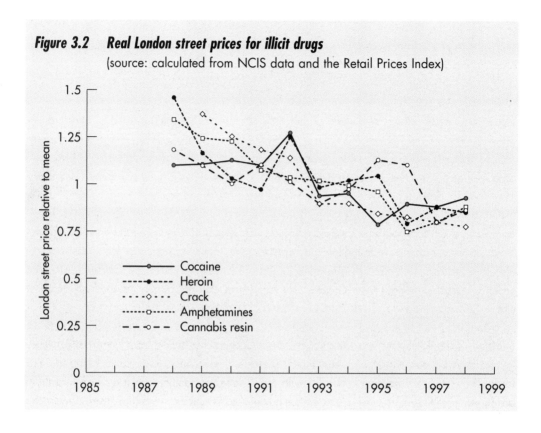

**Figure 3.2 Real London street prices for illicit drugs**
(source: calculated from NCIS data and the Retail Prices Index)

# 4      Evidence on individual patterns of drug use and offending

The first step is to carry out a simple analysis of each of the 17 drug/offending categories in turn. The results are given in Appendix Tables A1(a) to (f). Panels (a), (c) and (e) give estimates of the influence of personal characteristics on the hazards of drugs and offending. There are strong age effects and an extraneous rising trend linked to the index of availability. Local area characteristics also play a significant role, with deprived inner city areas being generally associated with increased hazards. As one might expect, females and those claiming some religious activity tend to have a lower risk of drug use and offending.

The 272 'gateway' coefficients are contained in panels (b), (d) and (f) of Table A1. For example, the coefficients in the cannabis row of panel A1(f) give the crude gateway effects of cannabis on the hard drugs. It is interesting to note that the only statistically significant impact for cannabis is on cocaine and that the magnitude of its impact is only slightly larger than that of alcohol. Table 4.1 summarises the pattern of crude gateway effects in schematic form. The pattern is weakly consistent with the gateway hypothesis in the sense that there are seven significant positive impacts of minor 'vices' on subsequent involvement in serious crime or consumption of the harder drugs cocaine, crack, heroin or methadone. However, only one of these (cannabis on cocaine) involves an illicit soft drug. It is striking that the group of 'minor' vices (tobacco, alcohol, cannabis, truancy and minor crime) tend to be associated with subsequent engagement in 'middle level' vices (amphetamines, ecstasy, LSD, magic mushrooms, tranquillisers, amyl nitrite) and to a lesser extent vice versa. The middle-rank drugs are more strongly linked to subsequent use of hard drugs.

## Table 4.1  The pattern of statistically significant 'gateway' responses

Impact on the hazard of onset for …

| Previous use of | Tob | Alc | Sol | Can | Tru | Min | Amp | Ecs | LSD | Mus | Tra | Amy | Coc | Cra | Her | Met | Ser |
|---|---|---|---|---|---|---|---|---|---|---|---|---|---|---|---|---|---|
| Tob |  | + | + | + | + | + | + | + | + | + |  | + |  | + |  |  |  |
| Alc | + |  | + | + |  | + | + | + | + | + | + | + | + |  |  |  | + |
| Sol |  |  |  | + |  |  | + |  | + |  |  | + |  |  |  |  |  |
| Can | + | + |  |  | + | + | + | + | + | + | + | + | + |  |  |  |  |
| Tru |  |  | + | + |  | + | + | + | + | + |  |  |  |  |  |  | + |
| Min | + | + | + | + | + |  | + |  | + |  | + | + | + |  |  |  | + |
| Amp |  |  |  |  |  | + |  | + | + | + | + | + | + | + |  |  | + |
| Ecs |  | − |  |  |  |  |  |  | + | − | + |  | + |  | + |  |  |
| LSD |  |  |  |  | + |  | + |  |  | + |  |  | + |  |  | + |  |
| Mus |  |  |  |  |  |  | + |  |  |  |  |  |  |  |  |  |  |
| Tra | − | + |  |  |  | + |  |  |  |  |  |  | + | + |  |  |  |
| Amy |  |  | + |  |  |  | + | + | + | + |  |  |  |  |  |  |  |
| Coc |  |  | + |  |  |  |  |  |  |  |  |  |  | + |  |  |  |
| Cra |  |  |  |  |  |  |  |  |  |  |  |  |  |  | + |  |  |
| Her |  |  |  | + |  |  |  |  |  |  | + |  | + |  |  | + |  |
| Met |  |  |  |  | + | − |  |  |  |  |  |  |  |  |  |  |  |
| Ser |  |  | + |  | + | + |  |  |  |  |  |  |  |  |  |  |  |

Notes: Tob, Alc, …, Ser refer to Tobacco, Alcohol, Solvents/glue, Cannabis, Truancy, Minor crime, Amphetamines, Ecstasy, LSD, Magic mushrooms, Tranquillisers, Amyl nitrite, Cocaine, Crack, Heroin, Methadone and Serious crime. "+" indicates a significant positive gateway, "−" indicates a significant negative gateway, at the 95% significance level.

It is not feasible to proceed with further modelling in full detail, since the computational demands would be enormous. Therefore a smaller number of composite categories need to be constructed. The construction of these categories is based on the information on age of onset in Table 2.1 and on the single equation results summarised in Table 4.1. Alcohol and tobacco are excluded from the analysis, since these are legal substances and unlikely ever to be made illegal. Secondly a distinction is maintained between solvents and other soft drugs because of the early age of onset for the former and thus its potentially important role in initiation to drug use. Ecstasy and cocaine are included in a single category because of their relatively high age of onset and their role as social drugs. This approach views cocaine as a drug with a much more socially acceptable image than heroin and crack.

The six categories finally specified are:

(i) *glue sniffing/solvent abuse;*

(ii) *soft drugs* (cannabis, amphetamines, LSD, magic mushrooms, tranquilisers, amyl nitrite);

(iii) *social drugs* (ecstasy or cocaine);

(iv) *hard drugs* (heroin, crack, methadone);

(v) *minor offending* (truancy, criminal damage, theft, dealing in stolen goods, cheque and credit card offences, fraud and affray); and

(vi) *serious crime* (theft of vehicles, robbery, burglary and assault).

## Controlling for unobservable confounding factors

The crude gateway effects, estimated in the previous part of this chapter, take no account of the possible confounding role of personal factors that are not reflected in the explanatory covariates summarised in Table 3.1. These unobservable factors might include aspects such as the family background or local economic and social environment that cannot be measured, or psychological attributes which predispose the individual towards problem behaviour of various kinds. From the perspective of the outside observer, these factors are distributed across individuals apparently randomly, but for each individual they act as a persistent factor affecting a broad spectrum of behaviour. Appendix Table A2(a) and (b) gives the detailed results of applying a statistical model based on this idea.

As in the more detailed model, the influence of observable personal characteristics and environment are as anticipated. Females and those with a religious affiliation have a generally reduced hazard of problem behaviour as, for the most part, do ethnic minorities. A disturbed family background or disadvantaged location increases the hazard. Age effects are strong, initially rising with age and then declining after a critical point. For the drug categories, the relevant macro-level index of availability captures the strong rising trend in drug use.

The implied pattern of gateway effects is summarised in Table 4.2. Having allowed for individual-specific unobservable confounding factors, these can be regarded as estimates of the direct 'true' causal gateways. There are several statistically significant impacts. Previous involvement in truancy or minor offending increases the risk of solvent abuse, whereas previous experience of soft and social drugs tends to reduce the risk of later substance abuse. There is significant evidence of a gateway from both solvent and soft drug abuse into cocaine/ecstasy use, while prior experience with hard drugs makes it less rather than more likely that there will be subsequent use of cocaine or ecstasy. Apart from these effects, the main gateways are (in both directions) between minor and serious offending.

**Table 4.2** **_The pattern of statistically significant gateway responses, corrected for unobservable confounding factors_**

| | | | Impact on the hazard of onset for ... | | | |
|---|---|---|---|---|---|---|
| | Solvents/ glue | Minor offending | Soft drugs | Social drugs | Hard drugs | Serious offending |
| Solvents/glue | | | | + | − | |
| Minor offending | + | | | | | + |
| Soft drugs | − | + | | + | | |
| Social drugs | − | | | | | |
| Hard drugs | | | | − | | |
| Serious offending | | + | | | | |

(Left axis label: Previous use of)

Notes: 'Minor offending' = truancy, criminal damage, theft, dealing, cheque and credit card offences, fraud, affray; 'Soft drugs' = cannabis amphetamines, LSD, magic mushrooms, tranquillisers, amyl nitrite; 'social drugs' = cocaine, ecstasy; 'Hard drugs' = crack, heroin, methadone; 'Serious offending' = theft of vehicles, robbery, burglary, assault. "+" indicates a significant positive gateway, "−" indicates a significant negative gateway, at the 95% significance level.

Besides these direct gateway effects, there may be indirect effects. For example, there is no significant evidence of a direct gateway from soft drugs into serious crime. However, soft drug use tends to increase the risk of minor offending, which in turn raises the hazard rate for serious offending. Thus Table 4.2 does not give a full picture of the pattern of causal links from past to current behaviour.

## Illustrating the role of observable and unobservable influences on behaviour

To provide a fuller quantitative assessment of behavioural gateways, the method of stochastic simulation is used. This involves taking the estimated transition model as a true description of behavioural processes and generating a large number (50,000 in this case) of hypothetical personal histories consistent with the random process that has been estimated from the YLS data. In outline, the procedure is as follows:

**Step 1** Choose a baseline individual type: white, male, with two working parents living in a non-deprived non-inner city neighbourhood, with general drug prevalence held fixed at low levels (10% soft drugs; 0.5% ecstasy/cocaine; 0.1% hard drugs).

**Step 2** Generate 50,000 different random individuals with the same baseline characteristics, but with randomly-differing values for the unobservable confounding factor, $u$.

**Step 3** For each year from age 11 to 30 in turn, generate drug/offending onsets at random according to the hazard levels predicted by the estimated model. Let these onset events feed forward into the hazard for the following year.

**Step 4** Calculate the proportion $(\hat{P})$ of the 50,000 simulated individuals with experience of each drug/offence category at some point in the generated history and the average age of onset $(\bar{\tau})$ for those who do become users/offenders.

**Step 5** Repeat the whole process for a version of the model estimated without allowance for unobservable effects and compare the results to assess the importance of these confounding factors.

**Step 6** Repeat the whole process again for each of a number of hypothetical individuals with observable characteristics differing from the baseline case, to indicate the impact that these characteristics have on drug use and offending rates. Four other hypothetical individuals were used:

(i)   a disadvantaged background (absent father, working mother, family history of trouble with police, resident in deprived inner-city area);

(ii)  female;

(iii) Asian;

(iv) a period of high drug prevalence (50% of the population having ever used soft drugs, 8% ecstasy/cocaine and 2% hard drugs).

For the baseline, Table 4.3 gives the proportion $(\hat{P})$ of the replications yielding experience of each drug or offence and the average age of onset $(\bar{\tau})$ in those cases. For the other four cases, the figures quoted are the difference $(\Delta\hat{P}, \Delta\bar{\tau})$ in prevalence and average onset age with respect to the baseline.

**Table 4.3**   **Predicted % prevalence ($\hat{P}$) and mean age of onset ($\bar{\tau}$) for baseline individual and differences relative to the baseline for other individual types (50,000 replications)**

| | | Solvents/ glue | Soft drugs | Cocaine & Ecstasy | Hard drugs | Minor offending | Serious offending |
|---|---|---|---|---|---|---|---|
| | | *Model estimated with observable variables only* | | | | | |
| Baseline white | $\hat{P}$ | 4.6 | 46.2 | 13.5 | 1.6 | 68.6 | 9.2 |
| male | $\bar{\tau}$ | 14.4 | 17.0 | 19.8 | 19.0 | 14.6 | 15.2 |
| Disadvantaged | $\Delta\hat{P}$ | +26.1 | +48.4 | +28.6 | +31.1 | +31.1 | +55.3 |
| | $\Delta\bar{\tau}$ | -0.4 | -1.6 | -0.5 | -2.1 | -2.1 | +0.1 |
| Female | $\Delta\hat{P}$ | -1.7 | -14.0 | -8.1 | -16.7 | -16.7 | -7.5 |
| | $\Delta\bar{\tau}$ | -0.2 | +0.1 | -0.1 | +0.2 | +0.2 | -0.5 |
| Asian | $\Delta\hat{P}$ | -2.2 | -34.0 | -10.7 | +0.5 | -20.7 | -4.1 |
| | $\Delta\bar{\tau}$ | -0.3 | +0.1 | -0.4 | -2.0 | +0.0 | -0.7 |
| Black | $\Delta\hat{P}$ | -3.7 | -19.2 | -8.5 | -1.2 | -2.2 | +4.8 |
| | $\Delta\bar{\tau}$ | -0.0 | +0.2 | -0.0 | -1.0 | -0.1 | -0.3 |
| High | $\Delta\hat{P}$ | +10.6 | +49.0 | +43.5 | +34.9 | +19.2 | +22.8 |
| prevalence | $\Delta\bar{\tau}$ | +0.5 | -1.8 | -0.8 | -0.0 | -0.1 | +0.9 |
| | | *Model estimated with additional random unobservable factor* | | | | | |
| Baseline white | $\hat{P}$ | 7.0 | 43.7 | 13.1 | 2.6 | 64.7 | 9.9 |
| male | $\bar{\tau}$ | 14.3 | 16.9 | 19.3 | 18.5 | 14.5 | 15.2 |
| Disadvantaged | $\Delta\hat{P}$ | +27.5 | +48.0 | +43.6 | +28.3 | +34.5 | +52.7 |
| | $\Delta\bar{\tau}$ | -0.6 | -2.3 | -1.7 | -1.7 | -2.2 | -0.9 |
| Female | $\Delta\hat{P}$ | -2.5 | -11.1 | -6.8 | -1.4 | -15.1 | -7.9 |
| | $\Delta\bar{\tau}$ | +0.1 | +0.3 | +0.4 | +0.1 | +0.3 | -0.0 |
| Asian | $\Delta\hat{P}$ | -2.4 | -30.0 | -10.1 | +0.4 | -18.9 | -4.7 |
| | $\Delta\bar{\tau}$ | +0.2 | +0.9 | +0.5 | -0.5 | +0.3 | -0.1 |
| Black | $\Delta\hat{P}$ | -4.5 | -15.5 | -9.1 | -2.0 | -1.2 | +3.9 |
| | $\Delta\bar{\tau}$ | +0.2 | +0.5 | +0.4 | +0.1 | +0.0 | +0.0 |
| High | $\Delta\hat{P}$ | +2.7 | +38.4 | +17.5 | +15.4 | +10.0 | +12.5 |
| prevalence | $\Delta\bar{\tau}$ | -0.1 | -1.5 | -0.7 | -1.1 | -0.2 | -0.2 |

A disadvantaged social/family background is clearly the dominant influence on drug use and offending, with general drug culture (as measured by prevalence) also extremely important. With the exception of a small but statistically significant rise in the hazard rate for serious crime for blacks, the influence of gender and ethnicity is to reduce the incidence of drug use and offending in comparison with the baseline white male group. In the case of ethnicity, these estimates are based on small sample numbers and therefore possibly are not very robust, but they suggest that common racial stereotypes of drug users are seriously in error. Comparing the two models estimated with and without allowance for unobservable confounding factors, there is a fair degree of robustness. Both sets of simulation results give a broadly similar picture of the influence of social, family and personal characteristics on the drugs/crime hazard.

Stochastic simulation is then used to assess the estimated size of the gateway effect. This is done by asking the question: "If a category of drug use or criminal activity could be completely removed, what effect would this have on the incidence of the other types of drug use or offending?" This is essentially a hypothetical question, used for the purposes of illustration, rather than a realistic possibility: not even the most optimistic policy-maker really believes that it would be possible to eliminate all soft drug use, for example. However, this kind of simulation can be informative. For example, if it showed that even a perfectly effective anti-soft drug policy would only have a small impact on hard drug use and serious crime, this would indicate that the gateway effect should not be seen as a major constraint on policy design.

Firstly, a complete offending history is simulated over the age range 11 to 30 for each individual in the YLS sample. Then the simulation is repeated, but with the hazard rate for one of the drug categories constrained to be zero. This is repeated for each category in turn; each set of results is then compared with the baseline in terms of prevalence among the simulated individuals and the average age of onset. Table 4.4 summarises the results produced using two versions of the transition model: one estimated with no allowance for random unobservable factors, the other including an individual-specific random factor. To make the results representative of the YLS target population, a fresh draw of the random factor u for each individual (held constant across all simulations for that individual) is used. Comparisons of the baseline and perturbed simulations give an assessment of the causal impact, or gateway effect, of each type of offending on other forms of offending, after controlling for the influence of unobservable confounding factors.

In both versions of the model, gateway effects are generally modest. For the version which ignores unobservable confounding factors, there are moderate gateway effects for truancy and minor crime. This implies that a policy, which could somehow end youth involvement in truancy and minor crime, would cut the incidence of drug use by around a quarter for soft drugs and half for other drugs. The only significant gateway effect of soft drugs is on ecstasy and cocaine, where there is a very large reduction from 11.7 per cent prevalence to 3.4 per cent prevalence; a reduction of more than two-thirds. After allowing for unobservable random effects, most of these impacts more or less disappear. The one remaining gateway effect any policy significance is the effect of soft drug use on subsequent use of ecstasy and cocaine. But even this is fairly small. The crude gateway effect is a cut of 8.3 percentage points from a base of 11.7 per cent prevalence. After correction for unobservable confounding factors, this becomes a cut of 3.8 percentage points. In other words, if all soft drug use could somehow be eliminated, the impact on use of ecstasy and powder cocaine would be a reduction of one-third. No conceivable policy on soft drugs is ever likely to reduce their incidence by more than a few per cent, so only a small fraction of this gateway reduction is plausible in practice. Conversely, given the already high prevalence of soft drugs among young people, it seems unlikely that the growth in prevalence arising from any relaxation of the law on soft drugs could be large enough to induce a major impact on hard drug use via the gateway effect.

**Table 4.4 Simulated impact of early experience of solvent abuse, soft drugs, truancy or crime on subsequent behaviour**

| Effect on use of ... | | Solvents/ glue | Soft drugs | Cocaine/ ecstasy | Hard drugs | Truancy | Serious crime |
|---|---|---|---|---|---|---|---|
| *Model estimated with observable variables only* | | | | | | | |
| Baseline case | $\hat{P}$ | 8.3 | 41.7 | 11.7 | 1.9 | 57.3 | 15.3 |
| | $\bar{\tau}$ | 15.3 | 16.8 | 19.3 | 19.0 | 14.3 | 15.4 |
| Effect of eliminating ... | | | | | | | |
| ... Solvents/glue | $\Delta\hat{P}$ | - | -1.8 | -0.9 | -0.3 | -0.5 | -0.3 |
| | $\Delta\bar{\tau}$ | - | +0.1 | -0.0 | -0.5 | -0.0 | -0.1 |
| ... Soft drugs | $\Delta\hat{P}$ | -0.9 | - | -8.3 | -1.3 | -3 | -1.2 |
| | $\Delta\bar{\tau}$ | -0.4 | - | -0.9 | -2.9 | -0.2 | -0.5 |
| ... Cocaine/ecstasy | $\Delta\hat{P}$ | +0.0 | -0.7 | - | -0.8 | -0.1 | -0.1 |
| | $\Delta\bar{\tau}$ | +0.0 | -0.0 | - | -1.9 | -0.0 | -0.1 |
| ... Hard drugs | $\Delta\hat{P}$ | -0.0 | -0.1 | -0.0 | - | -0.0 | -0.0 |
| | $\Delta\bar{\tau}$ | +0.0 | -0.0 | -0.0 | - | -0.0 | -0.1 |
| ... Truancy, minor crime | $\Delta\hat{P}$ | -4.1 | -10.8 | -5.0 | -0.9 | - | -4.6 |
| | $\Delta\bar{\tau}$ | -1.1 | -0.1 | -0.3 | -1.6 | - | -1.9 |
| ... Serious crime | $\Delta\hat{P}$ | -0.6 | -0.8 | -0.6 | -0.2 | -0.5 | - |
| | $\Delta\bar{\tau}$ | -0.1 | -0.0 | -0.0 | -0.2 | +0.0 | - |
| *Model estimated with additional random unobservable factor* | | | | | | | |
| Baseline case | $\hat{P}$ | 8.2 | 40.2 | 11.7 | 2.5 | 55.9 | 19.1 |
| | $\bar{\tau}$ | 14.1 | 16.7 | 19.2 | 17.9 | 14.0 | 14.9 |
| Effect of eliminating ... | | | | | | | |
| ... Solvents/glue | $\Delta\hat{P}$ | - | -0.2 | +1.1 | +0.6 | +0.0 | +0.1 |
| | $\Delta\bar{\tau}$ | - | +0.0 | -0.2 | +0.2 | +0.0 | +0.0 |
| ... Soft drugs | $\Delta\hat{P}$ | +0.7 | - | -3.8 | -0.2 | -0.6 | +0.2 |
| | $\Delta\bar{\tau}$ | +0.2 | - | -0.5 | -0.4 | -0.0 | +0.1 |
| ... Cocaine/ecstasy | $\Delta\hat{P}$ | +0.2 | +0.0 | - | -0.3 | +0.1 | +0.0 |
| | $\Delta\bar{\tau}$ | +0.0 | -0.0 | - | -0.6 | +0.0 | +0.0 |
| ... Hard drugs | $\Delta\hat{P}$ | +0.0 | +0.1 | +0.0 | - | +0.0 | +0.1 |
| | $\Delta\bar{\tau}$ | +0.0 | -0.0 | -0.0 | - | -0.0 | +0.1 |
| ... Truancy, minor crime | $\Delta\hat{P}$ | -2.0 | -1.3 | -1.3 | +0.8 | - | -3.3 |
| | $\Delta\bar{\tau}$ | -0.2 | +0.0 | +0.0 | +0.1 | - | -1.0 |
| ... Serious crime | $\Delta\hat{P}$ | -0.2 | +0.2 | +0.2 | +0.1 | -0.2 | - |
| | $\Delta\bar{\tau}$ | +0.0 | +0.0 | +0.0 | +0.2 | -0.0 | - |

# 5                                                                    Conclusions

There are several main conclusions to be drawn from this analysis.

It is dangerous to read too much into the empirical association between early soft drug use and subsequent hard drug use. It may well be that most hard drug addicts started off as soft drug users, but one cannot conclude from that fact that hard drug use is caused by previous experience of soft drugs. There may be many confounding social and psychological factors which are hard to observe and measure, and which simultaneously contribute to the drive towards both soft and hard drugs. Once an attempt is made to correct statistical estimates for the likely effects of these confounding factors, the implied gateway effects become much smaller.

The analysis, based on recent survey data on nearly 4,000 children and young adults, finds:

- No significant impact of soft drug use on the risk of later involvement with crack and heroin.
- Very little impact of soft drug use on the risk of later involvement in crime.
- A significant but small gateway effect probably exists linking soft drug use to the social drugs ecstasy and cocaine. However, after correcting for the likely effect of underlying unobservable factors, the predicted long-run consequence of even a complete removal of soft drugs from the scene would only be a one-third cut in the prevalence of ecstasy and cocaine.

The policy implications of gateway effects are not straightforward. Even if it is true that soft drug use increases the risk of later involvement in hard drugs and crime, this does not automatically justify the adoption of a strict policy on soft drugs. By linking soft and hard drugs under the same banner of illegality, a strict policy stance may have the perverse effect of amplifying the gateway effect and increasing the prevalence of hard drugs in the long run. Before translating empirical findings on the size of gateway effects into policy prescriptions, one must have a clear idea of how the gateway effect arises.

In any case, gateway effects are probably too small to be a major factor in the design of anti-drug policy. Other approaches, such as education, treatment and various types of local initiative, are more likely to be effective than a general campaign against soft drugs.

Social, economic and family circumstances seem to be the dominant influences on young people's risk of becoming involved in crime and drug use. Indirect policies, aimed at problems of local deprivation and family breakdown may offer at least as much hope as more direct anti-drug and anti-crime policies.

# Technical Appendix: Statistical Methods and Estimated Parameter Values

A discrete-time transition model is used, which is an analogue of the continuous-time transition model (see Lancaster (1990) and Mealli and Pudney (1996) for discussion). The discrete-time approach has several practical advantages in this case, since it can easily accommodate time-varying covariates, random confounding factors and non-proportional hazards. Other approaches are possible. For any given individual, consider an observation period that covers the years from some initial age $T_0$ to the current observed age $T_1$. Let there be $J$ different types of first-occurrence events. These events are the first use of each of the set of different drugs, the first episode of truancy and the first criminal offence of two types: minor and serious. Denote the ages at which these events occur by $\tau_1 \ldots \tau_J$. If event $j$ is not observed within the observation period, then $t_j$ is censored at the arbitrary value $T_1 + 1$.

## Single-equation modelling

Consider first the case of a single event type $j$, analysed in isolation. The analysis is conditioned on all other aspects of the individual's history and thus implicitly adopts a very simple view of causality. Define the hazard rate at age $t$ for event $j$ as the probability that event $j$ occurs at age $t$ conditional on no occurrence of the event prior to $t$. This probability is also conditional on the past history of the $J-1$ other event types. Let $x_{jt}$ be a vector of explanatory covariates relevant to event $j$ at time $t$. The vector $x_{jt}$ will in general contain variables describing aspects of the individual's history relevant to event $j$ and also the proxy for availability, $A_t$. The hazard rate is modelled as a conventional probit structure:

$$\Pr(\text{event } j \text{ occurs at age } t \mid \text{history}) = \Phi(x\beta_j) \tag{A1}$$

where $\Phi(.)$ is the cdf of the $N(0,1)$ distribution.

The case of independent random effects can be dealt with on a single-equation basis using standard software. The log-likelihood function for equation $j$ of this model is:

$$L(\beta_j) = \sum_{i=1}^{n} \ln\left[ \Phi(x_{j\tau_i}\beta_j) \prod_{t=T_0}^{\tau_{ij}-d_{ij}} [1-\Phi(x_{j\tau}\beta_j)] \right] \tag{A2}$$

where $d_{ij}$ is a binary indicator for uncensored observations such that $d_{ij} = 1$ if $\tau_{ij} \le T_1$ and $0$ if $t_{ij} > T_1$. Note that (A2) is the standard log-likelihood function for a probit model, estimated

29

from a set of $N = \Sigma_i\, (\tau_{ij} - T_0 + 1)$ observations. The relevant (log) prevalence variable is included as a covariate in the models for cannabis, amphetamines, ecstasy, LSD, cocaine, crack, heroin and methadone. For the remaining six substances and for truancy and crime, a quadratic time trend is used to approximate the effect of changing conditions over time. In every case where it is available, the use of the prevalence variable resulted in a better fit than the time trend. Full results for this model are given in Appendix Table A1[12].

## Joint estimation

The occurrences of events $1\ \dots\ J$ are assumed to be contemporaneously independent conditional on $x_{jt}$ and $u_j$. This still permits considerable dependence through lagged effects embodied in $x_{jt}$ and through correlation in the joint distribution of $u_1\ \dots\ u_j$. The probability of the observed joint event $\{\tau_1\ \dots\ \tau_J\}$ is:

$$\Pr(\tau_1\ _{\dots}\ \tau_j\,|\,X) = \int \mu(u)dG(u) \tag{A3}$$

where $\mu(u)$ is the conditional probability $\Pr(\tau_1\ _{\dots}\ \tau_j\,|\,X,u)$:

$$\mu(u) = \prod_{j=1}^{J}\left\{\prod_{t=1}^{\tau_j-d_j}\left[1-\Phi\left(x_{j_t}\beta_j + u_j\right)\right]\right\}\Phi\left(x_{j_{\tau_j}}\beta_j + u_j\right)^{d_j} \tag{A4}$$

where $X = \{x_{jt}, j = 1\ \dots\ J;\ t = 1\ \dots\ T\}$. The random effects $u = (u_1\ \dots\ u_J)$ are allowed to have different variances and to be cross-correlated. This is permitted by expressing the $u_j$ as linear combinations of a set of underlying independent standardised variates as follows:

$$u = R\epsilon \tag{A5}$$

where $R$ is a $J \times J$ loading matrix which is subject to a set of $J(J-1)/2$ normalising restrictions. $R$ is normalised to be a lower-triangular matrix, which is equivalent to working with the Choleski decomposition of the covariance matrix of the random vector $u$[13].

---

12  The single-equation results were computed using STATA 7.0; the quoted standard errors are calculated using robust formulae that take account of the clustering of years within individuals. Attempts to allow for Gaussian random effects within these single equation models were unsuccessful, since the random effects variances were estimated at zero in each case.

13  A formal analysis of the identifiability of this model is not given. However, the theoretical results of Abbring and van den Berg (2000) indicate that the identification of endogenous treatment effects is considerably less problematic in a duration setting than in the usual 2-period discrete response setting. In general, in their bivariate framework, nonparametric identification is achievable without the exclusion restrictions required in conventional selection models.

The parameters are estimated by maximising the following objective function, which is based on a second-order expansion of the log of the simulated likelihood function, with antithetic variate variance reduction[14].

$$\ln L = \sum_{i=1}^{n}\left[\ln(\bar{\mu}_i)+\frac{s_i^2}{2Q\bar{\mu}_i^2}\right] \tag{A5}$$

where $\bar{\mu}_i$ and $s_i^2$ are the mean and variance across replications of the $i$th likelihood element:

$$\bar{\mu}_i = \frac{1}{2Q}\sum_{q=1}^{Q}\left(\mu_i(\epsilon_{iq})+\mu_i(-\epsilon_{iq})\right) \tag{A6}$$

$$s_i^2 = \frac{1}{Q}\sum_{q=1}^{Q}\left[\frac{\left(\mu_i(\epsilon_{iq})+\mu_i(-\epsilon_{iq})\right)}{2}-\bar{\mu}_i\right]^2 \tag{A7}$$

where $\mu_i(\epsilon_{iq}) = \Pr(\tau_{i1} \dots \tau_{iJ} \mid X_i, \epsilon_{iq})$, $Q$ is the number of Monte Carlo replications used and $\epsilon_{iq}$ is a vector of independent pseudo-random variates drawn from the assumed standard normal distribution for $\epsilon$. This SML estimator is consistent and asymptotically normal with covariance matrix given by the usual inverse Hessian expression provided $Q$ goes to infinity at least as fast as $n$. $Q = 50$ replications are used in the calculations, which experience with similar models suggests is adequate to make SML approximate true ML reasonably closely (see Mealli and Pudney, 1996, for an example of this).

The SML estimator for this model is computationally demanding, so the strategy is to begin with the simplest 1-factor model in which $\epsilon$ contains a single random factor and the matrix $R$ is a column vector. Then a sequence of generalised models is estimated, with the number of random factors in $\epsilon$ increased by 1 at each step. This process is terminated when the addition of an extra factor leads to an insignificant improvement according to a simulated likelihood ratio criterion. In practice, the 1-factor model was preferred to the 2-factor by this criterion and the random effects estimates discussed below correspond to the 1-factor specification. In the 1-factor case, a comparison of the likelihood values computed at a representative point confirmed that this simulation approach delivers numerical accuracy comparable with the Gauss-Legendre quadrature used by Butler and Moffitt (1982) for an analogous multinomial probit model[15].

14  See Gouriéroux and Monfort 1996, page 45, but note the minor error in their equation 3.4.
15  If the result of 40-point quadrature is accepted as fully accurate, the simulation approach with Q = 50 gives a roughly similar degree of accuracy to 20-point quadrature. Standard statistical software often uses quadrature based on as few as 12 points.

**Table A1(a)  *Single-equation results for minor offences*** (standard errors in parentheses)

| Covariate | Tobacco | Alcohol | Glue | Cannabis | Truancy | Minor crime |
|---|---|---|---|---|---|---|
| Female | 0.095 | -0.086 | -0.066 | -0.150 | -0.081 | -0.317 |
| | (0.025) | (0.025) | (0.052) | (0.030) | (0.032) | (0.026) |
| Asian | -0.288 | -1.007 | 0.007 | -0.395 | -0.171 | -0.112 |
| | (0.069) | (0.081) | (0.134) | (0.117) | (0.092) | (0.073) |
| Black | -0.217 | -0.403 | -0.451 | -0.122 | -0.031 | 0.002 |
| | (0.076) | (0.084) | (0.218) | (0.121) | (0.097) | (0.091) |
| Religious | -0.176 | -0.055 | 0.091 | -0.095 | -0.172 | -0.065 |
| | (0.039) | (0.041) | (0.078) | (0.050) | (0.056) | (0.043) |
| Absent father | 0.084 | 0.139 | 0.064 | 0.118 | 0.181 | 0.115 |
| | (0.060) | (0.063) | (0.125) | (0.072) | (0.071) | (0.066) |
| Absent mother | 0.059 | -0.021 | -0.148 | 0.152 | 0.175 | -0.162 |
| | (0.108) | (0.102) | (0.203) | (0.122) | (0.126) | (0.121) |
| Working father | 0.058 | 0.180 | 0.008 | 0.020 | -0.148 | 0.034 |
| | (0.045) | (0.044) | (0.095) | (0.055) | (0.055) | (0.048) |
| Working mother | 0.003 | 0.060 | -0.041 | 0.107 | -0.068 | -0.000 |
| | (0.028) | (0.029) | (0.058) | (0.034) | (0.036) | (0.030) |
| Family trouble | 0.320 | 0.069 | 0.345 | 0.222 | 0.440 | 0.443 |
| | (0.116) | (0.102) | (0.141) | (0.120) | (0.122) | (0.098) |
| Inner city | -0.024 | -0.080 | 0.031 | 0.066 | 0.103 | 0.118 |
| | (0.030) | (0.031) | (0.065) | (0.037) | (0.039) | (0.033) |
| Deprived area | 0.061 | -0.116 | 0.169 | 0.107 | 0.133 | -0.059 |
| | (0.044) | (0.047) | (0.087) | (0.055) | (0.057) | (0.050) |
| Initial period | 0.498 | 0.950 | 0.421 | 0.179 | 0.339 | 0.230 |
| (up to age 11) | (0.054) | (0.076) | (0.156) | (0.105) | (0.195) | (0.057) |
| Age/10 | 33.09 | 27.80 | 44.10 | 20.96 | -163.0 | 5.295 |
| | (2.02) | (6.07) | (8.42) | (1.95) | (57.7) | (1.806) |
| $(Age/10)^2$ | -17.87 | -12.09 | -25.94 | -10.88 | 136.2 | -3.510 |
| | (1.10) | (3.78) | (4.67) | (1.02) | (41.5) | (0.968) |
| $(Age/10)^3$ | 2.978 | 1.459 | 4.625 | 1.727 | -36.87 | 0.630 |
| | (0.190) | (0.770) | (0.804) | (0.172) | (9.91) | (0.167) |
| Prevalence index | - | - | - | 0.570 | - | - |
| | | | | (0.035) | | |
| Time | -0.416 | -0.858 | 0.642 | - | 0.413 | -0.044 |
| | (0.114) | (0.116) | (0.255) | | (0.162) | (0.127) |
| $Time^2$ | 0.244 | 0.613 | -0.248 | - | -0.263 | 0.145 |
| | (0.052) | (0.053) | (0.112) | | (0.074) | (0.056) |

**Table A1(b)** **Single-equation results for minor offences** (standard errors in parentheses)

| Covariate | Tobacco | Alcohol | Glue | Cannabis | Truancy | Minor crime |
|---|---|---|---|---|---|---|
| Tobacco | - | 0.465 | 0.355 | 0.476 | 0.406 | 0.208 |
| | | (0.034) | (0.067) | (0.035) | (0.040) | (0.036) |
| Alcohol | 0.335 | - | 0.306 | 0.538 | 0.046 | 0.247 |
| | (0.034) | | (0.068) | (0.040) | (0.042) | (0.038) |
| Glue | -0.249 | 0.091 | - | 0.545 | 0.200 | 0.113 |
| | (0.150) | (0.140) | | (0.084) | (0.119) | (0.095) |
| Cannabis | 0.330 | 0.529 | 0.113 | - | 0.252 | 0.229 |
| | (0.099) | (0.142) | (0.102) | | (0.098) | (0.055) |
| Truancy | -0.019 | 0.087 | 0.292 | 0.115 | - | 0.164 |
| | (0.048) | (0.047) | (0.071) | (0.035) | | (0.038) |
| Minor crime | 0.152 | 0.302 | 0.396 | 0.247 | 0.221 | - |
| | (0.044) | (0.045) | (0.065) | (0.034) | (0.048) | |
| Amphetamines | -0.311 | -0.339 | 0.098 | 0.022 | 0.157 | 0.194 |
| | (0.185) | (0.371) | (0.185) | (0.174) | (0.245) | (0.090) |
| Ecstasy | 0.415 | -0.312 | -1.072 | -0.101 | 0.327 | -0.146 |
| | (0.236) | (0.364) | (0.380) | (0.352) | (0.481) | (0.143) |
| LSD | -0.319 | -0.499 | -0.322 | 0.334 | 0.006 | -0.183 |
| | (0.251) | (0.286) | (0.208) | (0.208) | (0.253) | (0.113) |
| Mushrooms | -0.078 | -0.052 | 0.323 | 0.209 | -0.049 | -0.068 |
| | (0.210) | (0.353) | (0.185) | (0.120) | (0.280) | (0.106) |
| Tranquillisers | -0.134 | -1.326 | 0.639 | 0.512 | -0.465 | 0.460 |
| | (0.375) | (0.635) | (0.267) | (0.458) | (0.413) | (0.185) |
| Amyl nitrite | 0.070 | 0.544 | 0.135 | 0.465 | -0.159 | 0.151 |
| | (0.147) | (0.339) | (0.150) | (0.089) | (0.191) | (0.083) |
| Cocaine | -0.195 | 0.027 | 0.650 | -0.480 | - | 0.140 |
| | (0.430) | (0.394) | (0.294) | (0.666) | | (0.165) |
| Crack | 0.267 | -0.472 | -0.591 | - | - | -0.050 |
| | (0.641) | (0.493) | (0.716) | | | (0.259) |
| Heroin | -0.660 | - | 0.485 | 0.636 | 0.913 | -0.484 |
| | (0.609) | | (0.521) | (0.493) | (0.274) | (0.328) |
| Methadone | 0.676 | - | -0.133 | 0.213 | 0.758 | - |
| | (0.637) | | (0.609) | (0.114) | (1.134) | |
| Serious crime | -0.136 | 0.218 | 0.273 | 0.029 | 0.117 | 0.404 |
| | (0.104) | (0.127) | (0.116) | (0.072) | (0.117) | (0.111) |

**Table A1(c)** **_Single-equation results for soft drugs_** (standard errors in parentheses)

| Covariate | Amphetamines | Ecstasy | LSD | Mushrooms | Tranquilliser's | Amyl Nitrate |
|---|---|---|---|---|---|---|
| Female | -0.133 | -0.244 | -0.201 | -0.371 | 0.022 | -0.195 |
| | (0.040) | (0.055) | (0.049) | (0.053) | (0.074) | (0.041) |
| Asian | - | -0.224 | -0.249 | -0.288 | 0.296 | -0.450 |
| | (0.341) | (0.252) | (0.241) | (0.258) | (0.248) | |
| Black | -0.328 | -0.082 | -0.892 | -0.501 | 0.018 | -0.131 |
| | (0.151) | (0.200) | (0.447) | (0.302) | (0.291) | (0.137) |
| Religious | -0.118 | 0.022 | -0.016 | 0.063 | -0.029 | -0.141 |
| | (0.071) | (0.090) | (0.088) | (0.089) | (0.127) | (0.075) |
| Absent father | -0.064 | -0.044 | 0.050 | -0.058 | 0.036 | 0.019 |
| | (0.098) | (0.129) | (0.104) | (0.115) | (0.140) | (0.106) |
| Absent mother | 0.158 | -0.098 | 0.141 | 0.209 | 0.316 | 0.157 |
| | (0.143) | (0.231) | (0.180) | (0.172) | (0.192) | (0.156) |
| Working father | -0.083 | -0.033 | -0.116 | -0.082 | -0.200 | 0.094 |
| | (0.072) | (0.097) | (0.084) | (0.088) | (0.115) | (0.080) |
| Working mother | 0.042 | 0.118 | 0.065 | -0.044 | 0.043 | -0.010 |
| | (0.044) | (0.064) | (0.057) | (0.055) | (0.086) | (0.045) |
| Family trouble | 0.233 | 0.054 | 0.031 | -0.111 | 0.066 | 0.040 |
| | (0.123) | (0.160) | (0.158) | (0.193) | (0.185) | (0.154) |
| Inner city | 0.042 | -0.057 | -0.003 | -0.013 | -0.103 | -0.011 |
| | (0.048) | (0.065) | (0.057) | (0.062) | (0.091) | (0.051) |
| Deprived area | 0.039 | 0.152 | -0.098 | -0.032 | 0.198 | 0.126 |
| | (0.069) | (0.002) | (0.091) | (0.093) | (0.116) | (0.070) |
| Initial period | -0.083 | - | - | -0.021 | -0.241 | -0.073 |
| (up to age 11) | (0.233) | | | (0.236) | (0.318) | (0.201) |
| Age/10 | 15.00 | 16.36 | 18.41 | 18.65 | 3.59 | 19.25 |
| | (2.76) | (4.28) | (3.37) | (3.55) | (4.73) | (2.69) |
| $(Age/10)^2$ | -7.55 | -7.78 | -9.26 | -9.81 | -2.15 | -10.24 |
| | (1.42) | (2.15) | (1.77) | (1.86) | (2.45) | (1.40) |
| $(Age/10)^3$ | 1.160 | 1.147 | 1.412 | 1.584 | 0.337 | 1.666 |
| | (0.230) | (0.351) | (0.302) | (0.318) | (0.411) | (0.236) |
| Prevalence index | 0.324 | 0.061 | 0.362 | - | - | - |
| | (0.035) | (0.011) | (0.053) | | | |
| Time | - | - | - | 1.316 | 1.592 | 2.832 |
| | | | | (0.380) | (0.757) | (0.422) |
| $Time^2$ | - | - | - | -0.570 | -0.474 | -1.017 |
| | | | | (0.152) | (0.279) | (0.159) |

**Table A1(d)** *Single-equation results for soft drugs* (standard errors in parentheses)

| Covariate | Ampheta-mines | Ecstasy | LSD | Mushrooms | Tranquill-iser's | Amyl Nitrite |
|---|---|---|---|---|---|---|
| Tobacco | 0.188 | 0.181 | 0.155 | 0.205 | -0.020 | 0.163 |
| | (0.051) | (0.077) | (0.063) | (0.068) | (0.105) | (0.052) |
| Alcohol | 0.476 | 0.481 | 0.210 | 0.221 | 0.373 | 0.525 |
| | (0.069) | (0.122) | (0.076) | (0.081) | (0.157) | (0.064) |
| Glue | 0.152 | -0.028 | -0.028 | 0.117 | 0.173 | 0.251 |
| | (0.072) | (0.087) | (0.079) | (0.084) | (0.095) | (0.074) |
| Cannabis | 0.577 | 0.460 | 0.559 | 0.439 | 0.572 | 0.452 |
| | (0.051) | (0.071) | (0.067) | (0.072) | (0.121) | (0.054) |
| Truancy | 0.241 | 0.120 | 0.151 | 0.202 | -0.021 | 0.045 |
| | (0.043) | (0.057) | (0.054) | (0.056) | (0.083) | (0.048) |
| Minor crime | 0.116 | 0.062 | 0.150 | 0.105 | 0.256 | 0.194 |
| | (0.044) | (0.058) | (0.055) | (0.057) | (0.086) | (0.046) |
| Amphetamines | - | 0.505 | 0.300 | 0.351 | 0.232 | 0.188 |
| | | (0.077) | (0.082) | (0.092) | (0.109) | (0.088) |
| Ecstasy | 0.345 | - | 0.290 | -0.279 | 0.259 | 0.008 |
| | (0.195) | | (0.136) | (0.141) | (0.115) | (0.133) |
| LSD | 0.553 | 0.347 | - | 0.235 | 0.181 | 0.054 |
| | (0.106) | (0.085) | | (0.109) | (0.109) | (0.109) |
| Mushrooms | 0.213 | -0.016 | 0.095 | - | 0.197 | -0.101 |
| | (0.093) | (0.091) | (0.100) | | (0.103) | (0.108) |
| Tranquillisers | 0.130 | 0.007 | -0.101 | -0.142 | - | 0.166 |
| | (0.163) | (0.151) | (0.165) | (0.175) | | (0.209) |
| Amyl nitrite | 0.281 | 0.178 | 0.324 | 0.230 | 0.145 | - |
| | (0.062) | (0.070) | (0.074) | (0.081) | (0.090) | |
| Cocaine | 0.132 | 0.186 | 0.031 | 0.151 | -0.193 | 0.002 |
| | (0.250) | (0.149) | (0.189) | (0.186) | (0.157) | (0.200) |
| Crack | - | 0.008 | 0.056 | -0.308 | -0.006 | -0.255 |
| | | (0.303) | (0.352) | (0.317) | (0.276) | (0.278) |
| Heroin | - | 0.218 | 0.265 | -0.514 | 0.986 | 0.185 |
| | | (0.289) | (0.321) | (0.454) | (0.253) | (0.280) |
| Methadone | 1.146 | -0.737 | 0.651 | - | 0.242 | -0.465 |
| | (0.477) | (0.334) | (0.569) | | (0.407) | (0.501) |
| Serious crime | 0.213 | -0.008 | 0.145 | 0.112 | 0.036 | 0.141 |
| | (0.077) | (0.094) | (0.088) | (0.089) | (0.109) | (0.078) |

## Table A1(e)   Single-equation results for hard drugs and serious crime
(standard errors in parentheses)

| Covariate | Cocaine | Crack | Heroin | Methadone | Serious crime |
|---|---|---|---|---|---|
| Female | -0.150 | -0.126 | 0.013 | 0.021 | -0.512 |
| | (0.068) | (0.116) | (0.135) | (0.158) | (0.053) |
| Asian | 0.278 | -0.804 | 0.465 | 0.557 | -0.048 |
| | (0.211) | (0.181) | (0.261) | (0.342) | (0.144) |
| Black | 0.038 | 0.081 | - | 0.492 | 0.239 |
| | (0.184) | (0.361) | | (0.342) | (0.129) |
| Religious | 0.086 | 0.070 | 0.085 | -0.077 | 0.004 |
| | (0.106) | (0.136) | (0.447) | (0.175) | (0.075) |
| Absent father | 0.063 | 0.025 | 0.368 | 0.357 | 0.122 |
| | (0.150) | (0.198) | (0.281) | (0.277) | (0.111) |
| Absent mother | -0.174 | 0.513 | 0.312 | 0.386 | -0.107 |
| | (0.257) | (0.214) | (0.339) | (0.355) | (0.214) |
| Working father | 0.139 | 0.129 | 0.576 | 0.321 | -0.057 |
| | (0.118) | (0.167) | (0.300) | (0.299) | (0.086) |
| Working mother | -0.129 | -0.039 | -0.107 | 0.056 | 0.029 |
| | (0.073) | (0.115) | (0.133) | (0.154) | (0.056) |
| Family trouble | 0.120 | -0.104 | -0.166 | 0.689 | 0.508 |
| | (0.187) | (0.278) | (0.269) | (0.200) | (0.118) |
| Inner city | 0.023 | 0.108 | 0.124 | -0.389 | 0.163 |
| | (0.072) | (0.119) | (0.137) | (0.149) | (0.056) |
| Deprived area | 0.199 | 0.281 | -0.055 | 0.557 | 0.019 |
| | (0.104) | (0.144) | (0.220) | (0.137) | (0.085) |
| Initial period | 0.833 | 0.075 | 0.413 | -0.147 | 0.510 |
| (up to age 11) | (0.296) | (0.363) | (0.366) | (0.375) | (0.108) |
| Age/10 | 14.68 | 9.79 | 35.07 | -6.19 | 15.38 |
| | (4.64) | (6.71) | (7.52) | (10.1) | (3.46) |
| $(Age/10)^2$ | -7.56 | -5.45 | -19.84 | 3.17 | -9.22 |
| | (2.28) | (3.37) | (3.83) | (5.30) | (1.85) |
| $(Age/10)^3$ | 1.228 | 0.886 | 3.423 | -0.590 | 1.632 |
| | (0.365) | (0.547) | (0.623) | (0.893) | (0.316) |
| Prevalence index | 0.226 | 0.109 | 0.241 | 0.279 | - |
| | (0.070) | (0.042) | (0.102) | (0.141) | |
| Time | - | - | - | - | -0.092 |
| | | | | | (0.233) |
| $Time^2$ | - | - | - | - | 0.167 |
| | | | | | (0.100) |

**Table A1(f)**  **Single-equation results for hard drugs and serious crime**
(standard errors in parentheses)

| Covariate | Cocaine | Crack | Heroin | Methadone | Serious crime |
|---|---|---|---|---|---|
| Tobacco | 0.182 | 0.425 | 0.097 | -0.102 | 0.118 |
| | (0.099) | (0.148) | (0.194) | (0.226) | (0.068) |
| Alcohol | 0.335 | 0.313 | 0.219 | -0.013 | 0.199 |
| | (0.161) | (0.237) | (0.214) | (0.327) | (0.078) |
| Glue | 0.086 | 0.031 | 0.214 | -0.014 | 0.117 |
| | (0.086) | (0.159) | (0.168) | (0.194) | (0.096) |
| Cannabis | 0.446 | -0.020 | 0.086 | 0.452 | 0.063 |
| | (0.095) | (0.164) | (0.243) | (0.330) | (0.088) |
| Truancy | 0.010 | 0.242 | 0.142 | 0.037 | 0.275 |
| | (0.070) | (0.133) | (0.170) | (0.176) | (0.065) |
| Minor crime | 0.211 | -0.101 | 0.160 | 0.261 | 0.595 |
| | (0.073) | (0.128) | (0.162) | (0.218) | (0.063) |
| Amphetamines | 0.539 | 0.543 | 0.505 | -0.036 | 0.274 |
| | (0.097) | (0.219) | (0.272) | (0.253) | (0.112) |
| Ecstasy | 0.449 | 0.121 | 0.564 | 0.004 | -0.041 |
| | (0.091) | (0.183) | (0.208) | (0.194) | (0.140) |
| LSD | 0.273 | 0.135 | 0.345 | 0.626 | 0.079 |
| | (0.091) | (0.182) | (0.215) | (0.189) | (0.122) |
| Mushrooms | 0.092 | 0.218 | -0.063 | 0.154 | 0.013 |
| | (0.086) | (0.146) | (0.198) | (0.152) | (0.110) |
| Tranquillisers | 0.110 | 0.425 | 0.618 | 0.245 | 0.100 |
| | (0.134) | (0.172) | (0.201) | (0.215) | (0.207) |
| Amyl nitrite | 0.113 | 0.164 | 0.219 | 0.213 | -0.025 |
| | (0.080) | (0.159) | (0.195) | (0.232) | (0.102) |
| Cocaine | - | 0.587 | 0.220 | -0.010 | 0.033 |
| | | (0.159) | (0.203) | (0.220) | (0.189) |
| Crack | 0.220 | - | 0.784 | -0.403 | -0.001 |
| | (0.366) | | (0.263) | (0.423) | (0.246) |
| Heroin | -0.317 | 0.940 | - | 1.373 | 0.199 |
| | (0.329) | (0.272) | | (0.294) | (0.297) |
| Methadone | 0.252 | -0.344 | 0.210 | - | 0.122 |
| | (0.385) | (0.395) | (0.454) | | (0.342) |
| Serious crime | -0.132 | -0.080 | 0.185 | 0.099 | - |
| | (0.094) | (0.163) | (0.172) | (0.204) | |

### Table A2(a)  Results for the multivariate random-effects model
(standard errors in parentheses)

| Covariate | Solvents | Soft | Cocaine/E | Hard | Truancy, etc. | Serious crime |
|---|---|---|---|---|---|---|
| Female | -0.212 | -0.305 | -0.550 | -0.426 | -0.255 | -0.624 |
| | (0.076) | (0.046) | (0.083) | (0.156) | (0.029) | (0.064) |
| Asian | -0.183 | -0.940 | -0.848 | -0.015 | -0.311 | -0.146 |
| | (0.225) | (0.175) | (0.412) | (0.546) | (0.079) | (0.174) |
| Black | -0.599 | -0.405 | -0.823 | -0.732 | -0.000 | 0.184 |
| | (0.259) | (0.135) | (0.379) | (0.980) | (0.087) | (0.155) |
| Religious | 0.051 | -0.213 | 0.005 | -0.120 | -0.196 | -0.030 |
| | (0.113) | (0.073) | (0.131) | (0.281) | (0.045) | (0.096) |
| Absent father | 0.358 | 0.380 | 0.300 | 0.246 | 0.173 | 0.232 |
| | (0.147) | (0.096) | (0.168) | (0.338) | (0.064) | (0.113) |
| Absent mother | -0.171 | 0.329 | 0.197 | 0.542 | 0.093 | -0.129 |
| | (0.270) | (0.174) | (0.269) | (0.437) | (0.125) | (0.253) |
| Working father | 0.078 | 0.087 | 0.128 | 0.153 | -0.075 | -0.049 |
| | (0.112) | (0.074) | (0.128) | (0.271) | (0.048) | (0.088) |
| Working mother | 0.017 | 0.151 | 0.119 | 0.026 | -0.008 | 0.095 |
| | (0.074) | (0.050) | (0.080) | (0.156) | (0.032) | (0.060) |
| Family trouble | 0.844 | 0.837 | 1.015 | 0.999 | 0.723 | 0.783 |
| | (0.202) | (0.163) | (0.245) | (0.374) | (0.102) | (0.149) |
| Inner city | 0.068 | 0.074 | 0.146 | 0.182 | 0.112 | 0.206 |
| | (0.082) | (0.052) | (0.086) | (0.175) | (0.035) | (0.064) |
| Deprived area | 0.136 | 0.097 | 0.262 | 0.285 | 0.079 | 0.009 |
| | (0.122) | (0.079) | (0.122) | (0.228) | (0.051) | (0.089) |
| Initial period | 0.497 | 0.092 | 0.790 | 0.281 | 0.387 | 0.604 |
| (up to age 11) | (0.179) | (0.133) | (0.401) | (0.486) | (0.061) | (0.140) |
| Age/10 | 43.62 | 26.11 | 21.36 | 15.35 | 26.76 | 15.39 |
| | (5.49) | (2.44) | (4.77) | (9.53) | (1.97) | (3.95) |
| $(Age/10)^2$ | -23.84 | -11.69 | -8.592 | -6.899 | -14.38 | -8.376 |
| | (3.01) | (1.24) | (2.284) | (4.945) | (1.08) | (2.110) |
| $(Age/10)^3$ | 4.035 | 1.634 | 1.074 | 0.974 | 2.397 | 1.387 |
| | (0.535) | (0.205) | (0.360) | (0.841) | (0.190) | (0.364) |
| Prevalence index | - | 0.704 | 0.258 | 0.476 | - | - |
| | | (0.053) | (0.047) | (0.182) | | |
| Time | 0.227 | - | - | - | 0.054 | -0.169 |
| | (0.359) | | | | (0.131) | (0.287) |
| $Time^2$ | -0.054 | - | - | - | 0.021 | 0.218 |
| | (0.149) | | | | (0.056) | (0.118) |

### Table A2(b)  Results for the multivariate random-effects model: estimated effects of prior offending history and of random effects (standard errors in parentheses)

| Prior use of ... | Effect on the risk of onset for ... | | | | | |
| --- | --- | --- | --- | --- | --- | --- |
| | Solvents | Soft | Cocaine/E | Hard | Truancy, etc. | Serious crime |
| ... solvents | - | 0.196 | 0.527 | -0.375 | -0.002 | -0.053 |
| | | (0.106) | (0.113) | (0.184) | (0.130) | (0.109) |
| ... soft drugs | -0.240 | - | 0.399 | 0.061 | 0.127 | -0.034 |
| | (0.095) | | (0.079) | (0.230) | (0.058) | (0.088) |
| ... cocaine / E | -0.533 | 0.023 | - | 0.229 | -0.181 | -0.033 |
| | (0.338) | (0.364) | | (0.160) | (0.139) | (0.140) |
| ... hard drugs | 0.005 | -0.327 | -0.606 | - | -0.389 | -0.245 |
| | (0.352) | (0.451) | (0.239) | | (0.439) | (0.281) |
| ... truancy, etc. | 0.347 | 0.093 | -0.078 | -0.162 | - | 0.440 |
| | (0.073) | (0.049) | (0.092) | (0.170) | | (0.068) |
| ... serious crime | 0.104 | -0.136 | -0.207 | -0.052 | 0.233 | - |
| | (0.119) | (0.105) | (0.106) | (0.162) | (0.118) | |
| | Scale parameters for random effects (R) | | | | | |
| | 0.874 | 0.885 | 1.123 | 1.215 | 0.403 | 0.468 |
| | (0.100) | (0.065) | (0.142) | (0.231) | (0.032) | (0.071) |

# References

Abbring, J.H. and Van der Berg, G.J. (2002). *The non-parametric identification of treatment effects in duration models.* Working paper, Free University Amsterdam.

Advisory Council on the Misuse of Drugs (2002). *The Classification of Cannabis under the Misuse of Drugs Act (1971).* London: Home Office.

Aldridge, J., Parker, H. and Measham, F. (1999). *Drug trying and drug use across adolescence. A longitudinal study of young people's drug taking in two regions of northern England.* London: Home Office, DPAS Paper no. 1.

Brock, W. and Durlauf, S. (2000). Interactions-based models, in *Handbook of Econometrics*, vol. 5, J. Heckman and E. Leamer (eds.). Amsterdam: North-Holland.

Butler, J. S. and Moffitt, R. (1982). A Computationally Efficient Quadrature Procedure for the One-Factor Multinomial Probit Model, *Econometrica*, 50, 761-764.

Fergusson, D. M. and Horwood, L. J. (2000). Does cannabis use encourage other forms of illicit drug use? *Addiction* 95, 505-520.

Flood-Page, C., Campbell, S., Harrington, V. and Miller, J. (2000). *Youth Crime: Findings from the 1998/99 Youth Lifestyles Survey.* London: Home Office Research Study no. 209.

Gourieroux, C. and Monfort, A. (1996) Simulation-Based Econometric Methods. Oxford: Oxford University Press.

Kandel, D. B. and Yamaguchi, K. (1993). From beer to crack: developmental patterns of drug involvement, *American Journal of Public Health* 83, 851-855.

Kenkel, D., Mathios, A. D. and Pacula, R. L. (2001). Economics of youth drug use, addiction and gateway effects, *Addiction* 96, 151-164.

Lancaster, T. (1990). *The Econometric Analysis of Transition Data.* Cambridge: Cambridge University Press.

Manski, C. F. (1993). Identification of social effects: the reflection problem, *Review of Economic Studies* 60, 531-542.

Manski, C. F. (2000). Economic analysis of social interactions, *Journal of Economic Perspectives* 14, 115-136.

Mealli, F. and Pudney, S. E. (1996). Occupational Pensions and Job Mobility in Britain: Estimation of a Random-Effects Competing Risks Model, *Journal of Applied Econometrics* 11, 293-320.

Metropolitan Police Service (2002). Evaluation of Lambeth's pilot of warnings for possession of cannabis - summary of final report. London: MPS Consultancy Group report.

Pacula, R. (1997). The modelling of the gateway effect, *Health Economics* 6, 521-524.

Pudney, S. E. (2001).The growth of illicit drugs markets in the UK 1978-99. University of Leicester: Discussion Papers in Public Sector Economics no. 01.

Pudney, S. E. (2002). Keeping off the grass? An econometric model of cannabis consumption by young people in Britain. University of Leicester: Discussion Papers in Economics no. 02.

Stratford, N. and Roth, W. (1999). *The 1998 Youth Lifestyles Survey Technical Report*, London: National Centre for Social Research.

UKADCU (2000). *United Kingdom Anti-Drugs Co-ordinator's Second National Plan 2000/2001*. London: Cabinet Office.

Van Ours. J. C. (2001). Is cannabis a stepping-stone for cocaine? University of Tilburg: CentER Discussion Paper no. 2001-98.

Van Ours, J. C. (2002). A pint a day is good for your pay but smoking takes the gain away. University of Tilburg: CentER Discussion Paper.

Yamaguchi, K. and Kandel, D. B. (1984a). Patterns of drug use from adolescence to young adulthood II. Sequences of progression, *American Journal of Public Health* 74, 668-672.

Yamaguchi, K. and Kandel, D. B. (1984b). Patterns of drug use from adolescence to young adulthood III. Predictors of progression, *American Journal of Public Health* 74, 673-681.

# RDS Publications

## Requests for Publications

Copies of our publications and a list of those currently available may be obtained from:

Home Office
Research, Development and Statistics Directorate
Communication Development Unit
Room 275, Home Office
50 Queen Anne's Gate
London SW1H 9AT
Telephone:     020 7273 2084 (answerphone outside of office hours)
Facsimile:     020 7222 0211
E-mail:        publications.rds@homeoffice.gsi.gov.uk

alternatively

why not visit the RDS website at
        Internet: http://www.homeoffice.gov.uk/rds/index.html

where many of our publications are available to be read on screen or downloaded for printing.